Making Lily Laugh!

By Ellen Dreyer
Illustrated by Amy Wummer

Modern Curriculum Press
Parsippany, New Jersey

Cover and book design by Liz Kril and Design 5

Modern Curriculum Press
An imprint of Pearson Learning
299 Jefferson Road, P.O. Box 480
Parsippany, NJ 07054–0480

www.pearsonlearning.com

1-800-321-3106

ISBN 0-7652-0891-1

4 5 6 7 8 9 10 11 12 13   MA   07 06 05 04 03 02 01 00

Contents

For my nieces, Hilary, Laura, Marielle, and Melanie, who make me laugh

CHAPTER

1

Lily, the Alarm Clock

"Waaaaaaaaaaaaaa!"

Roy's legs started to move under the covers. They moved back and forth as though he were running.

"Waaaaaaaaaaaa-aaaaaaaaa!"

Roy turned over in bed and put the pillow on his head. What was that noise anyway? Was he dreaming? Was it a fire truck siren? What else could it be?

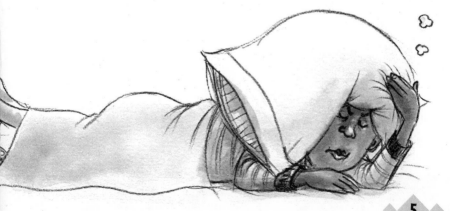

LILY!

Roy opened one eye and looked at his alarm. It read 6:30 A.M.

"Oh, no," Roy thought. "I wish I were dreaming. Now I have to listen to another day of Lily's crying."

He tumbled out of bed and stretched. Then he walked down the hall to his baby sister Lily's room. There he found his mother holding Lily.

"You're up early, Roy," Mom whispered, giving him a kiss on the forehead.

"Who needs an alarm clock, when I have Lily?" he whispered back. When he peeked at Lily, he smiled. Her eyes were starting to close. Maybe he could go back to bed for another half-hour.

Just then Roy's grandmother came to the door. "Well, good morning, big brother," she said, giving Roy a hug. Then Roy's mom handed Lily to her.

"Thanks," Roy's mom said. She went to get ready for work.

"Gran," Roy asked, keeping his voice low, "how come Lily cries so much?"

"She's teething," Gran said. "She'll calm down once her teeth come in."

"When will that be?" Roy asked.

"A few months, give or take a few weeks. Every baby is a little different," she replied.

Gran leaned over Lily's crib and laid her down on her back. Suddenly, Lily's eyes opened. Her lips trembled. She opened her mouth....

"WAAAAAAAAAAAAAAA!"

"There goes my extra half-hour," Roy groaned. He leaned over the crib and started to gently rub her head. She used to love that. Now it didn't help.

"It's OK, Roy," Gran said, patting his shoulder. "You go get ready for school."

Roy headed back to his room.

"Morning, champ," Roy's dad called out from the open bathroom door. "I'll make pancakes this morning," he said.

"Great!" Roy said. Pancakes were his second-favorite food, right after pizza.

Roy quickly washed, brushed his teeth, and got dressed. After grabbing his books, he headed down to the kitchen.

At the bottom of the stairs, he made a quick stop in the room his mom and dad used as an office. He remembered that his mom had set out a book for him to use for a school project.

Roy's mom was a teacher. Her desk was piled with books and papers and other school stuff. The book was right on top.

Roy's dad worked at the Presto toy factory in town. His desk was covered with toy stuff, such as plastic eyeballs, metal springs, and "giggle chips." The giggle chips were little sound disks put into dolls to make them laugh.

Roy picked up one of the giggle chips. As he turned it over, a high, silly laugh came out of it. "I've got to ask Dad how these things are made," Roy said to himself.

By the time he got to the kitchen, Roy's stomach was growling. His dad was standing at the stove, flipping pancakes.

"Maybe this will take your mind off Lily's crying," Mr. West said. He rolled his eyes at Roy as he put a plate of pancakes in front of him.

Then Roy's dad reached into the refrigerator and took out a baby's teething ring. "I'm going to run upstairs and give this to Gran," he said. "Maybe it's cool enough to make Lily's gums feel better."

"Probably not," Roy glumly thought.

CHAPTER

2

A Friend in Need

After breakfast, Roy put on his coat and grabbed his book bag. "Bye!" he called. No one heard him. He gathered up his things and went out the door.

It was a gray, cold day. "Maybe it'll snow today," Roy thought. "Then Julie and I could go sledding in Sumner Park." Julie Sands was one of his best friends. He usually stopped by Julie's apartment so they could walk together to school.

At Julie's building, he rang the buzzer to her apartment. As he ran up the stairs, he thought, "I could use a friend today."

The second the door opened, Julie's dog,
Ruff, jumped up on Roy. She licked his face.
"Down, girl. Down!" Julie cried.

Julie's mom was at the breakfast table.
"Want a muffin?" she asked as Roy came in.

"No, thanks," Roy replied. "Dad just
made me pancakes."

He looked around the table. Julie calmly buttered her muffin. Mrs. Sands calmly sipped her coffee. "Wow! Everything is so calm here," Roy said. "I don't hear any crying babies," he added.

"How is that cute baby sister of yours?" Mrs. Sands asked.

Roy shook his head. "She's teething."

"That hurts, doesn't it?" Julie asked.

"Yes, I guess it does," Roy replied.

"I remember when Julie was teething," Mrs. Sands said. "A cold teething ring was the only thing that helped."

"That works for about ten seconds with Lily," Roy said.

"Hey, we'd better go," Julie said. She kissed her mom.

Roy and Julie headed up the street.

"If it snows today, do you want to go sledding in the park this afternoon?" Roy asked Julie.

Julie looked at Roy. "How come you never ask me over to your house after school anymore?" she asked.

"Lately my house sounds like police sirens and fire truck sirens all going off at the same time," Roy sighed.

"Sounds like fun," Julie said.

"You don't want to come over. It's too noisy," Roy said.

They walked in silence until they reached the corner. The crossing guard held them back.

"Lily used to be such a happy baby," Roy told Julie as they waited. "I could always get her to giggle."

"I'll help you get her giggling again," Julie said.

"No way. Nobody can," Roy said.

"Hey, I'm an inventor. It's my job to solve problems," Julie said.

"I remember the thing you made with paper clips to fish your sunglasses out of the toilet," Roy said.

"That was the Paper-Clip Dipper," Julie added. They both started to laugh.

"If you can solve *this* problem," Roy said, "you will be more than an inventor. You will be a *genius.*"

CHAPTER 3

A Friend Indeed

After the 3:00 bell rang that afternoon, Roy met Julie in the schoolyard. A little snow was falling, but there wasn't enough on the ground to go sledding.

"Do you want to come over to my house?" Roy asked Julie.

"I thought you didn't want me to come to your house," Julie said.

"Well, if you can put up with the crying, you can come over," Roy replied.

"All right, but let's stop at my place first," she said.

When they got to Julie's apartment, Julie called for Ruff. The big collie came running, wagging her tail.

"This is my newest invention," Julie said.

"Ruff, your dog, is an invention?" Roy asked, laughing.

Julie found Ruff's dog brush and started brushing her hard. Roy could hear a faint crackling sound as Julie pulled the brush over the dog's fur. In a couple of minutes, Ruff's fur stood straight out from her body.

"Now watch," Julie said. She started to put little pieces of notepaper all over Ruff. The notes stuck to her fur like nails to a magnet. Ruff began to parade around.

"I call it the Walking Reminder," Julie said proudly. "The brushing builds up a lot of static in Ruff's fur. That's an electrical charge caused by the brushing. It's just like when we walk with socks on a carpet and our hair stands on end. It makes her the perfect bulletin board. When I want to check a note, I just pull it off her fur."

Roy wrote out a note. It said, "Julie is a nut." Then he stuck it on Ruff.

"Who knows?" Julie said, giggling. "I may be a *famous* nut someday."

"I bet you will," Roy said. "I think I'll do better if I stick to computers, though."

He looked around the room. "Hey, isn't that Piggy?" he said as he picked up a stuffed pig from a chair.

"That's right. It's the exact same pig you got when we were in kindergarten," Julie replied. "I put it on my desk when I do my homework. It helps me think better."

"I gave mine to Lily," Roy said. "She loves it. Well, she *used* to love it. Even Piggy can't make her laugh now."

Julie stared at Piggy. "Hmmm," she said. "Let's take Piggy for a ride." She put the jolly pink pig in her school backpack.

At Roy's house, Gran was having a cup of coffee in the kitchen. Roy gave her a kiss, and Julie hugged her. Then they sat at the table with her.

"Mrs. West," Julie said. "Roy and I are going to baby-sit for Lily."

"*What?*" Roy replied, looking surprised.

"That's sweet of you two," said Gran. "Lily has been fussy all afternoon. This is the first time she has been quiet. I could use a break from baby-sitting."

Julie nodded. "Great idea."

As Gran left the kitchen, Roy stared at Julie. "What did you say that for?"

Waaaaaa!

"This is it," Julie said, leading Roy upstairs. "It's time for Operation Lily Laugh."

As soon as they passed Lily's room, they heard her rustling in her crib.

"Here it comes," Roy stopped. "It's time for Operation Lily Cry."

"Wa...wa...waaaa...WAAAAAAAAAA!"

"Pick her up," Julie said above the noise.

Roy stepped into the baby's room and lifted her out of the crib. Lily's crying became quieter but did not stop.

"Rock her," Julie directed.

Roy sat in the rocker next to the crib and started moving back and forth.

"I'll sing," Julie said, and she started singing "Old MacDonald Had a Farm."

Lily kept crying.

Then Julie made funny faces and funny sounds. She even marched around, then put her hands on her sides. She laughed big, deep laughs. "Ho, ho, ho!" she said.

Nothing worked. Lily cried until she fell asleep in Roy's arms. Roy was afraid to move for fear he would wake her again.

"Don't worry," Julie said. "I've got an idea."

A Pig Idea

Finally, Roy slowly rocked forward and got out of the chair. Then, he carefully walked over to the crib and gently laid Lily down. Luckily, she kept on sleeping.

"Where's Lily's pig?" Julie whispered. Roy pointed to the end of the crib.

Julie picked up the pig, making sure she didn't disturb Lily. They left the pig in Roy's room, then went back down to the kitchen.

In the kitchen, Julie took her pig out of her backpack. "What if we made a deluxe-o pig that is sure to make her laugh?" she asked.

"What are you talking about?" Roy said.

"We'll take the stuffing out of my pig and put a water balloon inside. Then we'll glue it back together," Julie explained.

"Yeah, then what happens?" Roy asked, puzzled.

"We give it to Lily, silly. Do you have any balloons and glue?" Julie asked.

Roy was getting more and more curious about Julie's idea. "I think so," he said. "My dad might have some of that stuff in the office. He has lots of things in there he uses to make some of his toy ideas into models. He lets me use whatever I want."

They went to the office and quickly found the stuff they needed. They even found a few extra goodies to make the pig really special.

Gran was coming down the stairs as Roy and Julie were running back to the kitchen. "What are you two doing?" she asked.

"We're going to make Lily laugh," Roy grinned, "or Julie is. I'm just the helper."

"So, I assume I'm to go back to watching Lily until you're finished?" Gran asked.

"Please, Gran," Roy said.

"Well, don't make a mess in the kitchen," she smiled.

"Don't worry, Gran," Roy and Julie replied. "We'll clean up after ourselves."

As Gran went back up the stairs, she said, "I don't see how a pile of junk can make a teething baby laugh. If Julie can do that, she should get the Inventor of the Year award!"

Pig Unstuffed

Roy and Julie dumped the stuff on the kitchen table.

"Let's get started," Roy said.

Julie held her pig in front of her and sighed. "OK, Pig, it's been great playing with you," she said. "Now you've got an important job to do."

"You can change your mind," Roy told her. "It isn't too late."

"No," Julie said. "It's OK." She took the scissors and cut through the cloth on the pig's belly.

"Owwwww," Roy groaned softly.

Julie glared at Roy. "OK, wise guy. Please fill the balloon."

Roy put the balloon under the kitchen faucet. It filled up quickly, too quickly. The water splashed out of the top of the balloon. Then the balloon slipped out of Roy's hands and plopped on the floor. Water spilled everywhere!

First, Roy tried to mop up the water with a dish towel. When the towel became quickly soaked, he had to get the mop. Julie was so busy taking the eyes off of the pig, she didn't even notice what had happened.

"Why do I always listen to Julie's crazy ideas?" Roy thought.

After he put the mop away, he tried again. This time he was careful not to fill the balloon all the way. He tied it off with a knot and carried it over to the table.

Roy watched while Julie put the water balloon inside the pig's body. The pig began to wiggle and wobble.

"After I put the glue on, you hold the two sides of the belly together," she said.

"Yes, doctor," Roy replied with a smile.

Julie put a line of glue on one side of the cloth on the pig's belly. Then Roy pulled the two sides together and pressed the unglued side down over the strip of glue.

"Don't press too hard," Julie said, "or you'll break the balloon."

"I'm being careful," Roy replied.

"Keep holding the sides together while I give the eyes a little action," Julie said.

She cut two small strips off one end of a kitchen sponge. Then she glued a goggle eye onto one side of each sponge strip. Finally, she glued the strips to the places where the pig's eyes had been. The large goggle eyes bobbed a little.

Roy gently let go of the pig's body. The glue held as the water balloon inside the body jiggled. "This is one wiggler of a pig," Roy said.

Julie laughed. "It's a Piggler!" she said.

The Piggler

"Do you think this Piggler will work?" Roy asked.

"Let's hope so," Julie said, as they both heard Lily crying loudly upstairs.

They quickly cleaned the stuffing off the floor and picked up the supplies they had used. They finished just as Gran came through the kitchen.

"So, how's that miracle invention coming along?" asked Gran.

"Great," Julie said. "Right, Roy?"

Roy held up the Piggler. Gran stopped talking and stared at the jiggling pig.

"Anything that can leave me with nothing to say is quite an invention," she finally said. "Let's hope it has the same effect on Lily," she added.

Waaaaaaaaaa!

Gran smiled and went up the stairs.

Just then Mrs. West came home from work.

"Well, Julie Sands, I haven't seen you in quite some time," Roy's mom said.

"Hi, Mrs. West," Julie replied.

Before Mrs. West saw the Piggler in Julie's hands, she heard Lily crying. "Is that Lily?" she asked.

"Who else?" Roy said. "Gran just went up to get her."

Roy's mom headed for the stairs. "I'll go give her a hand," she said.

As she left the room, Roy's dad came home. As he put down his briefcase, he looked up toward the ceiling.

"WAAAAAAAAAAAAAA!"

"Sounds like we're going to have another noisy night," he sighed. "I'll get another teething ring out of the refrigerator."

"Let's go, too," Julie said. "It's time for the Piggler to make its first appearance."

Julie and Roy followed Mr. Sands up the stairs. When they got to Lily's door, they saw Roy's mom holding Lily. His dad was holding out the teething ring for Lily to take. Lily kept right on crying.

"Oh, baby, poor baby," said Roy's mom.

"Show the Piggler to Lily," Julie whispered to Roy.

"Do you think it will work?" Roy whispered back, holding the Piggler.

"We won't know unless we try it," Julie replied.

Roy stepped into Lily's room. He brought the Piggler out.

"Lily," he said. "We have a surprise for you. Look."

Roy held up the Piggler as he walked forward. The pig's body jiggled and wobbled. It even made a wonderful sloshing sound as Roy walked.

Lily's teary eyes turned to look at Roy. Then her eyes looked down and saw the Piggler.

CHAPTER 7

A Good Try

For a few seconds nothing changed. Lily just looked at the Piggler while tears ran down her face. Then, something amazing happened. Lily stopped crying. She smiled and reached for the Piggler.

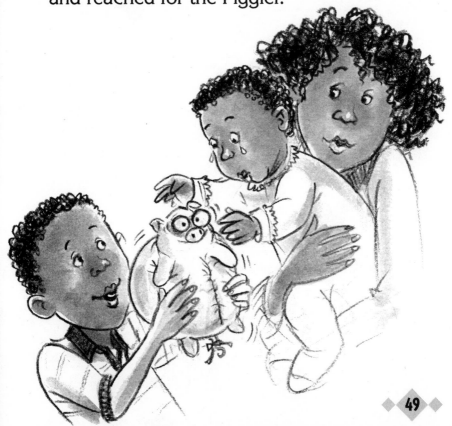

Roy started to give the Piggler to Lily. He wanted her to see how funny the toy was, so he squeezed and shook the Piggler as he held it out. The pig jiggled and wobbled even more. The goggle eyes goggled.

Then Roy squeezed too hard. The seam on the Piggler's belly split. The balloon broke. Water splashed and spilled.

Lily looked up at her brother as water dripped from his chin and down his shirt. Then, her smile got bigger and wider. She started to laugh.

"Oh, Roy," Gran laughed. "Your invention worked...somewhat."

At first, Roy's parents looked puzzled. Then, they started to laugh, too. Finally, even Roy started to grin.

But Lily soon stopped laughing. Her eyes began to fill with tears again.

"Oh, no," Roy moaned as Lily's giggles turned to wails.

"That was a good try," his mom said kindly as she handed Lily to Gran. "Why don't you go get some rags and clean up this mess? I'll get dinner started."

Roy handed the popped Piggler to Julie. He grabbed some rags from the hall closet and cleaned up the water.

Julie began to help Roy. "We're not finished yet," she said.

Try, Try Again

Roy stared at Julie. "No, thanks. One disaster a day is enough for me."

"Just listen," Julie said. "We can start again. Come on, I'll show you."

They went into Roy's room, and Julie pulled Lily's pig out from its hiding place. "Look!" she said. "We'll use this."

Roy shook his head. "Noooooo. That's the only pig left. And Lily loves it!"

Julie sighed. "All right. No more water balloons. What else does Lily like?" she asked.

"She likes her bottle, she likes me to rub her head, she likes it when any of us talks to her," Roy said.

"That's it!" Julie said. "She likes voices. What if the Piggler could talk?"

"That's impossible!" Roy replied. Then he thought about it. As he looked at Lily's pig, he thought of the giggle chips.

"Wait a second," he told Julie. "I think I've got just the thing that will work." He was sure his dad wouldn't mind if he borrowed a couple of chips.

"I'll be right back," he said, and he ran downstairs to his parents' office.

"OK," he said to Julie as he came back into the room. He put the pig on his desk and picked up the scissors.

"What are you doing?" she said.

"Just watch," Roy told her. He made a tiny cut on the pig's chest seam. He slid two of the giggle chips inside. Then he glued the opening shut.

"What are those?" Julie asked.

"Giggle chips," he explained.

When he finished, he turned the pig right-side up. A giggling sound came out.

Julie's face lit up. "Hey, you're a better inventor than you think!" she said.

Heehee
hee
hee
hee !!

CHAPTER 9

Piggler Has
the Last Laugh

Roy and Julie marched back into Lily's
room. Mom, Dad, and Gran stared at them.
"You're not going to try that water
balloon trick again, are you?" Gran asked.

"No," Roy said, and went over to Lily's crib. "Hey, Lily," he said. "Look at this."

Lily looked up at the new Piggler. She stopped crying.

As Lily watched, Roy made the pig dance. Lily still did not smile.

Then Roy squeezed the pig's chest. It giggled. Lily looked a little startled. Then, she smiled a little.

Roy kept dancing the pig around the crib. Then, he squeezed it again. It giggled again. Lily made a little giggle of her own. She smiled wider this time. The pig giggled again. Lily laughed again.

Finally, Lily reached for the pig and hugged it. Roy showed her how to squeeze it. Lily began to laugh.

"I can't believe it," Gran whispered.

Lily just kept squeezing the pig. Each time she did, it giggled, and she laughed.

Ha ha ha !!

"What do you call this toy?" Roy's
dad asked.

"It used to be a Piggler," said Roy. "Now
it's a Giggler."

"It's a Piggler Giggler! This is a great
idea." Dad smiled proudly. "I'm going to
have to tell Presto Toys about this one!"

"Even the best inventors have some wacky ideas," Julie said. "And if you try hard enough and use your head, an idea just might work."

"And sometimes two heads are better than one!" Roy added.

"And as I said before, anyone who could make Lily laugh deserves the Inventor of the Year award," Gran said. "Or Inventors of the Year," she added.

They all looked at Lily. She was tightly hugging the Piggler and laughing right along with the pig.

Ha ha ha

Hee hee hee

Glossary

appearance (uh PIHR uns) the act of coming into sight; the way a thing looks

assume (uh SOOM) to suppose something is a fact

effect (e FEKT) a result; an event caused by another event

genius (JEEN yus) a person with high mental ability or brainpower

goggle (GAHG ul) pushing out or bulging

inventor (ihn VEN tur) a person who is the first to think of and make something

magnet (MAG niht) a stone or piece of metal that can attract iron or steel

miracle (MIHR uh kul) an amazing thing or happening

model (MAHD ul) a small object made to serve as a plan for a larger, final object

static (STAT ihk) electric disturbance in the air that can cause a mild spark or shock